TABLE OF CONTENTS

CHOWDERS, STEWS and SOUPS

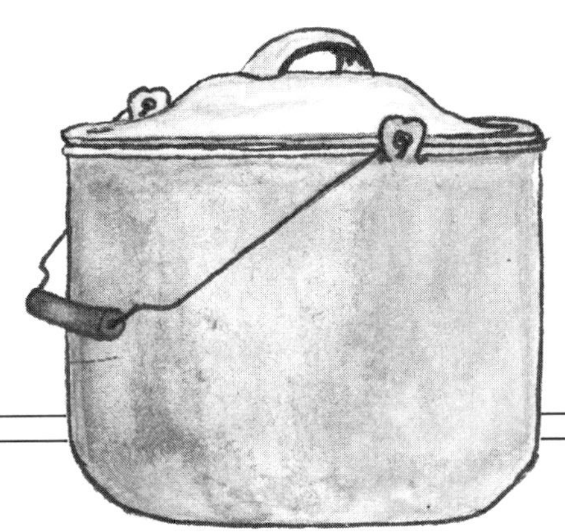

In Maine, we consider a soup kettle a necessary part of our kitchen equipment. Just as important are recipes that go into these chowder kettles.

The heavy black iron soup kettles Maine housewives used long ago are just about gone from the local scene. We use the flat-bottomed shiny variety with tight-fitting covers because we now do our cooking on a surface unit. No longer can most of us push the soup kettle to the back of the stove. But in Maine homes where this is possible, then you're apt to find one of the heavy black soup kettles.

We prepare our clam stew, lobster stew, fish chowder, corn chowder, beef stew and similar Maine recipes for which we are famous in very much the same old way.

In many years of writing the newspaper column "Cooking Down East," I have learned these are the recipes you want to use in your own homes.

It makes us aware that an old Maine recipe is just as much of an heirloom as a lovely antique.

MAINE LOBSTER STEW

Boil 2 one-pound Maine lobsters and remove meat immediately, saving also the tomalley (or liver), the coral and the thick white substance from inside the shell. Using a heavy kettle, simmer the tomalley and coral in ½ cup butter for about 8 minutes. Then add lobster meat cut in fairly large pieces. Cook all together slowly using a low heat for about 10 minutes. Remove from heat or push to back of stove and cool slightly. Then add very slowly, 1 quart rich milk, stirring constantly. Allow the stew to stand, refrigerated, 5 or 6 hours before reheating for serving. This is one of the secrets of truly fine flavor. It's called aging. Serves 4.

You do not need salt or pepper when the stew is prepared in this manner. For the perfect lobster stew: Stirring is the most important thing in this masterpiece, otherwise it will curdle. According to experts on fine Maine cookery, the important steps to success in creating the perfect lobster stew are, first, this partial cooling before ever so gently adding the milk —a mere trickle at a time. The constant stirring until the stew blossoms a rich salmon color under your spoon and, finally, the aging, since every passing hour improves its flavor. Some "experts" even say two days, overnight is good and 5 to 6 hours improves its flavor considerably. Be sure to reheat slowly.

SHRIMP STEW

Using our Maine shrimp in a stew is a fine way of preparing this delicacy. Because we like to serve these shrimp at their best, it is wise to use raw shrimp in making a stew for the best flavor. Maine shrimp do not need to be deveined.

Use peeled raw Maine shrimp, cook in butter just as you would in making any Maine stew. Do this slowly, the shrimp are cooked when they lose their glassiness and curl up. This takes about 2 or 3 minutes.

Add milk slowly. Heat to boiling point, add salt and pepper to taste.

CLAM STEW

For each portion use 1 dozen small, tender Maine clams shucked out raw and 1½ cups milk. Saute clams in frying pan in their own juice, adding butter. Heat milk in top part of double boiler. Combine sauted clams and milk. Season to taste. Serve immediately.

★A quahog or quahaug, if you prefer that spelling, is a hard-shelled round clam. Large quahogs are known as "Chowders", medium-sized quahogs are called "Cherry-stones" and small quahogs are "Littlenecks". It is cherry-stones and littlenecks that taste so good "on the halfshell", they're just the right size for eating raw.

QUAHOG STEW

½ cup butter
1 pint shucked quahogs with liquor
1 quart milk, or 3 cups milk and 1 cup light cream
¼ teaspoon black pepper
½ teaspoon salt

Scald the milk. While it is heating, melt the butter in a saucepan. Add the raw quahogs, which have been chopped fine and the liquor to the melted butter. Cut up the quahogs by placing them on a small wooden board and with a paring knife cut each one into several small pieces. Simmer the butter, chopped raw quahogs and liquor together about 3 minutes. Add to heated milk. Add salt and pepper. Taste, to be sure of seasoning. Serve at once with crackers. Serves 4.

Quahog stew can be made in exactly the same way if you use steamed quahogs. In other words, if you have steamed the quahogs to open them, then remove the cooked quahogs from the shells and chop the quahogs into small pieces. Use about ½ cup of the broth with the chopped quahogs in the melted butter and simmer this all together for 3 minutes, before adding it to the heated milk.

Quahogs are excellent used in a chowder and it is made exactly as you would make clam chowder; just be sure you chop the quahogs before adding them to the chowder.

SCALLOP STEW

1 pound scallops
¼ cup butter
1 quart milk
Salt and pepper to taste
½ tablespoon Worcestershire sauce

Melt butter in soup kettle, cut raw scallops in bite-size pieces, cook slowly in melted butter. They are cooked as soon as they turn white. Remember to cook all fish "short", overcooking toughens all fish. Add milk slowly, stirring as you do so. Add Worcestershire sauce, salt and pepper to taste. Heat. Keep in mind that a scallop stew is a little on the sweet side, yet a delicious stew that is a rare treat. It is a rich stew. This recipe serves 4.

OYSTER STEW

1 pint oysters
1½ pints to 1 quart milk
6 tablespoons butter
1 tablespoon Worcestershire sauce
½ teaspoon celery salt
Salt to season, after stew is made
½ to 1 teaspoon paprika

Put raw oysters in saucepan. Add butter and seasonings. Stir and bring quickly to a boil, lower heat, continue stirring and cooking not longer than 2 minutes, allowing edges of oysters to curl. Add milk, bring again to just below boiling point, but do not allow to boil (or it could curdle). Dip into bowls, add another piece of butter to each bowl if you wish, sprinkle with paprika. Serve with oyster crackers. This serves 2 amply. If you use a quart of milk it will serve 4 skimpily.

MAINE CLAM CHOWDER

1 quart fresh Maine clams, shucked raw
2 thin slices salt pork
1 small onion, diced in small pieces
4 cups diced (small) potatoes
1 cup water or enough to just show up through the potatoes
Salt and pepper
1½ quarts milk
1 tall can evaporated milk
Piece of butter
Common crackers

Using a kettle, fry out salt pork using a low heat. Remove pork and cook diced onion slowly in fat, taking care not to burn it. Add the four cups diced potatoes and the water, better add a little salt and pepper right now. Cover kettle, bring to steaming point, lower heat, cook until potatoes are soft, about 15 minutes.

In the meantime, using cutting board and a sharp knife, cut the head of each clam in two or three pieces. Do the same with the firm part of the clam and the soft part or bellies, also. No, I do not remove the black part. Save any juice you can.

When potatoes are soft, stir in the cut clams, cover pan again, let cook for 3 minutes, no longer for it toughens the clams. Add 1½ quarts of milk and the evaporated milk. Taste for seasoning, add salt and pepper if necessary. Keep in mind that as the chowder ripens it may be salty enough. Add piece of butter or margarine.

The old recipes always advised us to allow chowder to ripen in refrigerator several hours or a day. Then to reheat it slowly over a very low heat. But now that we use homogenized milk the ripening period often is omitted to avoid danger of the chowder separating, a problem sometimes associated with use of homogenized milk. The use of evaporated milk, as given in these recipes, also helps to avoid curdling.

Serve chowder with common crackers, pilot crackers or Maine blueberry muffins. Serves six.

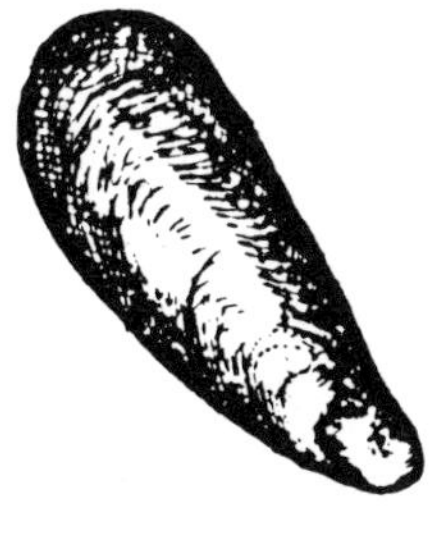

FISH CHOWDER
With Old Fashioned Flavor

¼ pound salt pork, diced
2 onions, sliced or diced
4 cups potatoes, in small pieces
1 or 2 cups water
2 pounds fish fillets (haddock, cod or cusk)
1 teaspoon salt
¼ teaspoon pepper
¼ teaspoon Accent
2 or 3 cups whole milk
1 tall can evaporated milk

Fry diced salt pork slowly in bottom of heavy kettle until golden colored. Remove pork scraps and set aside. There should be about 3 tablespoons fat in the kettle. Add onions and cook until yellowed (but not brown). Add potatoes and enough water so it comes nearly to top of potatoes. Place fish on top of potatoes, sprinkle with seasonings. Cover, bring to a boil, then cook on low heat until potatoes are tender and the fish "flakes." Pour in both kinds of milk and allow to heat thoroughly but not boil. Serves 6.

If you do any stirring at all, be gentle, because fish should be in fairly large pieces, not flaked apart and certainly not "mushed".

Good old Maine custom dictates that reheated pork bits be scattered on top of chowder. But you may serve them in a separate dish in case someone votes against the idea.

★Salmon chowder is a traditional chowder in Maine. It harks back to days when meat was not always on hand and fresh fish not available. This recipe has filled a need in Maine since olden days. It might be a good idea for you to have a can of salmon in your cupboard, just for an emergency.

SALMON CHOWDER

2 slices salt pork
3 or 4 slices onion, diced
3 cups diced potatoes
Salt and pepper
1 cup water
1 tall can salmon
1 quart milk
Lump of butter

Cook slices of salt pork until fat is "tried out". Cook onion until golden in fat after removing pork slices. Add water to kettle, add raw potato, salt and pepper. Cover kettle and bring to steaming point. Cook on low heat about 15 minutes or until potato is tender.

Use pink, medium or red salmon. The buying public has come to think of red salmon as the only first class salmon, but this is not the case. Pink salmon used in this chowder is delicious and a lot less expensive.

Break up canned salmon, removing skin and bones. Leave salmon in as large chunks as possible. Add salmon and liquor to kettle. Stir lightly, add milk. Add piece of butter or margarine. Taste for seasoning. If you prefer, a half stick of margarine may be used as the fat for cooking onion in place of the salt pork.

The longer this chowder ages, the better. You will like its pink color. Serve with common crackers if available.

★ It happened when Horace Hildreth was Governor of Maine. Maine cooks were asked to submit their favorite seafood recipes. The response was heartwarming. I was one of the judges for that contest. It was the sort of happening one could never forget. This Crabmeat Stew was a winner then and it still is.

CRABMEAT STEW

2 tablespoons butter
6 small soda crackers
2 cups fresh crabmeat
½ cup water
1 quart milk
Salt and pepper
1 tall can evaporated milk

Melt butter slowly in kettle. Roll crackers until crumbs are as fine as flour. Place these crumbs and the crabmeat in butter, add water, and let mixture bubble for one minute to bring out the luscious flavor of the crabmeat. Pour in the milk and stir until it is very hot, but do not boil. Add seasonings and evaporated milk. Reheat, but again do not boil. Serves 6.

★ I've had my fair share of judging recipe contests and am very grateful for the opportunity. Not so many years ago, the Maine Dairy Council sponsored Maine Grange Dairy suppers during June — Dairy Month. I recall that the first time that we did it, 153 Maine granges entered this contest. Huntoon Hill Grange of Wiscasset won that first contest. Their main dish which was strictly Maine was for Lobster Chowder. It was the first time I had known of lobster being used in a chowder.

LOBSTER CHOWDER

6 to 8 tablespoons butter
2 small onions, minced
4 medium sized potatoes, diced
Salt and pepper to taste
4 medium sized lobsters, or when cooked and picked out, enough to make 1 pound lobster meat
2 quarts milk, warmed

Cook the onion and potato in one cup water in a covered pan until they are tender. Add cooked lobster meat that has been cut into smallish pieces. Add butter. Stir with a fork to mix together and cook about 3 minutes. Warm the milk, then add to the lobster mixture. Season to taste. Allow to mellow. Serves 6 to 8.

SEAFOOD CHOWDER

2 slices salt pork
1 small onion, diced
2 cups water or bottled clam juice
3 cups pared and diced potatoes
1 pound haddock fillets
Salt and pepper
½ pound scallops
1 pint chopped clams, or 2 cans minced clams
1 can crabmeat or
2 cups fresh lobster meat or
2 cups Maine shrimp
2 quarts milk, scalded
1 stick butter or margarine

Fry out salt pork in kettle, remove pork scraps and cook diced onion in fat, gently. Add water or clam juice, potatoes, cover and cook about 15 minutes. Lay haddock fillets and fresh scallops on top of potatoes, simmer slowly just until fish "flakes" and scallops are done. It is best to quarter the scallops before placing them in kettle. If clams are uncooked, then they go into kettle at same time. If canned clams are used, then they are added with crabmeat, cooked lobster meat and cooked shrimp. Add scalded milk, stick of butter or margarine. Taste for seasoning. This chowder will be enough for 8 to 10 people.

Once the chowder is assembled, the top of double boiler is excellent for keeping until serving time and leaves far less chance of any curdling or "separation." This holds for any stew or chowder where milk is involved.

★ Easy Maine Style Clam Chowder is easily prepared from ingredients you have stored in your cupboard. It has a delicious flavor and you will exclaim, "This is second best to a chowder made with fresh Maine clams."

MAINE STYLE CLAM CHOWDER

3 slices salt pork
1 small onion, diced
One 8-ounce bottle clam juice
3 cups diced raw potatoes
Black pepper to taste
Two 8-ounce cans minced clams or whole clams
3 cups milk or one 14½-ounce can evaporated milk, plus 1 can water
Salt to taste
½ stick butter or margarine

Using a deep saucepan, fry salt pork slowly, remove and add diced onion. Cook on low heat until onion is soft. Add clam juice, diced raw potato and enough black pepper to satisfy your taste. Cover pan, bring to steaming point. Lower heat and cook at least 15 minutes.

Remove cover, add minced clams including juice, stir to mix. Cook about 10 minutes with cover off, allowing clams to simmer along in cooked potato mixture. Add milk, butter or margarine, heat to serving point. Taste for seasoning, add salt and more pepper as needed. Serves 4 to 6. If you wish, cut pieces of lightly browned salt pork into small bits and sprinkle on top of bowls of chowder before serving.

SHELLFISH

Clams/Scallops/Oysters Shrimp/Crab/Lobster

CLAMS

★I never saw anyone who enjoyed digging clams, getting them ready for steaming, serving and eating them any more than my Dad. None of it ever seemed any bother to him. You were practically eating them once the idea of clams had been suggested. He liked doing it himself, too. Didn't want women folks bothering around at all. He knew at just what point the oval, thin-shelled Maine clams were ready. He relied on no one else's judgment. Neither did we!

The heaping soup plates of steamed clams, opened like butterflies, would be passed to us as we filed by the kitchen stove and into the dining room. The clam water bouillon was served scalding hot in sturdy cups. Small dishes of melted butter were at each place and it was a feast. Only home-made bread and butter was needed to complete it. Sour pickles helped. And coffee.

STEAMED CLAMS

Scrub clams well with a stiff brush. Be sure they are rinsed carefully to get rid of that last bit of mud or sand. Do each clam separately is a good rule for delicious steamed clams. Place clams in a large kettle and add cold water, but only enough to cover the bottom of the kettle. Otherwise how do you expect to get true clam water? The general rule is one-half cup cold water to each four quarts of clams in the shell. Cover tightly. Bring to steaming point. Cook over low heat for 10 to 20 minutes or until shells open. To test for doneness? No better way than eating one, hot as it is! Serve with melted butter. And clam water.

FRIED CLAMS

1 egg, separated
½ cup milk
¼ teaspoon salt
1 tablespoon melted butter
½ cup sifted all-purpose flour
1 pint shucked raw Maine clams

Separate egg, beat egg white until stiff. Add milk, salt and melted butter to the egg yolk and beat together. Add sifted flour and stir. Fold in the stiffly beaten egg white.

Drain clams and dip each clam into batter and fry in deep fat at 375 degrees until golden brown. Drain on absorbent paper.

CLAM CAKES

1 pint chopped clams
1½ cups cracker crumbs
2 eggs, unbeaten

Mix clams and crumbs together. Add eggs one at a time and mix well. Let stand for a few minutes to soften crumbs. Mixture should hold together and be moist.

Fry in butter in a frypan. Drop in large spoonfuls of the mixture, press down with spoon to make cakes ¾ inch thick. Fry on one side until brown, turn and brown other side. If common crackers are used, season with salt. Do not add salt if saltines are used. The liquid from the clams may be used and adds flavor.

★ Because we have such good canned minced clams, some of our favorite casseroles are made with them rather than fresh clams.

NEW CLAM CASSEROLE

1 can minced clams
30 salty crackers crushed
2 eggs, beaten
1 cup milk
1 can cream of mushroom soup
¼ cup melted butter or margarine

Beat the 2 eggs, slightly. Add cream of mushroom soup, milk, crackers, clams and butter. Turn into a greased 1½ quart casserole. Bake at 350 degrees for 1 hour. I like to place any casserole which uses eggs and milk into a pie plate, with about ½ inch hot water in plate. It helps to prevent curdling.

★ Old-fashioned Clam Pie is sometimes made with potatoes, but most Maine cooks favor a clam pie that has nothing that takes away from the delicate clam flavor. Preferably, you will use fresh clams in making this delicious old Maine recipe.

OLD-FASHIONED CLAM PIE

Pastry for a 2-crust pie
1 pint fresh clams
2 slices salt pork
1 slice onion, minced
Salt and pepper
1 tablespoon flour or enough to thicken clam mixture

Use a spider and try out the salt pork, remove pork scraps. Add small amount of onion, cook until soft. Chop clams, not too fine. Add to fat and onion, cook gently about 5 minutes. Add flour to thicken; make certain mixture is hot. Add salt and pepper to taste.

Using 9-inch pie plate, line with pastry. When I turn a hot filling into a lower pastry, I like to have the top all rolled, ready to place over filling. Turn filling into pastry. Cut 3 slits in top pastry, place on pie. Flute edges. Bake at 400 degrees 15 minutes; lower to 325 degrees, continue baking about 25 minutes longer. Serve very hot. Serves 4.

CLAM WHIFFLE

12 single saltine crackers
1 cup milk
2 eggs, beaten
¼ cup butter or margarine, melted
One 7-ounce can minced clams
¼ teaspoon Worcestershire sauce
1 teaspoon chopped green pepper
2 teaspoons chopped onion
Dash of salt and pepper

Crumble crackers and soak in milk for a few minutes, combine with other ingredients, adding beaten eggs last. Pour into greased 1½ quart casserole, place in shallow pan of hot water. Bake at 350 degrees, uncovered, for 40 minutes. Serves 4.

★ Having canned minced clams in your cupboard means you can do interesting things like stuffed clams. Or you could make a clam whiffle. You will find it good insurance against any kind of weather to have them on hand.

STUFFED CLAMS

Serves 2

One 7-ounce can minced clams
Same amount freshly rolled cracker crumbs, measured in can
2/3 stick margarine
1 teaspoon Worcestershire sauce
Pepper

Melt margarine, add to crumbs. Drain clams and mix with buttered crumbs. Add Worcestershire sauce and pepper, taste for seasoning, add salt if you wish. Spoon into shells or small shallow casseroles. This will make a supper dish for 2. If served for a first course, use smaller shells and this amount will serve 4. Bake at 350 degrees for 20 minutes.

★ Scalloped oysters are always a treat. This recipe from our Winthrop friend whose cooking is well known in this part of Maine says the recipe was given to her by an elderly friend, a long time ago. Like everyone else, you are sure to agree this is a very special recipe.

SCALLOPED OYSTERS

1 pint oysters, drained, save 2 tablespoons liquor
½ cup dried bread crumbs
1 cup rolled cracker crumbs
¼ cup melted butter
Salt and pepper
1 tablespoon sherry
1 tablespoon cream
Buttered crumbs for top

Mix crumbs with butter, using a fork. Butter an 11 x 7-inch casserole. Place thin layer crumbs in bottom, then a layer of oysters. Add salt and pepper, more crumbs, oysters, then top with crumbs. In case you do not have enough crumbs for top, then do a few more.

Using a knife, make holes down through layers, taking care not to mix layers. Mix oyster liquor, naturally you will use all of it; just make certain you have 2 tablespoons. Using an egg beater (yes even for this small amount) beat liquor, sherry and cream. Pour mixture into holes. Bake at 400 degrees for 20 minutes. Serves 4.

★"A pint's a pound the world around!" Remember when we used to say that? It isn't exactly true but with scallops it is. Some fishermen sell them by the pint and some sell them by the pound. Either a pint or a pound of scallops is enough for four people. The simplest ways to cook them are usually best.

BAKED SCALLOPS

Put margarine to melt in a shallow pan. (Use a shallow glass baking dish). Wash scallops and dry them.

Put bread crumbs or cracker crumbs into a pie plate. First, roll dried scallops in melted margarine, then roll in crumbs, then place back in shallow baking dish in which margarine was melted. (You will get the benefit of all this melted fat, in this way).

Continue, until all scallops are prepared. Place scallops separately so they will bake quickly.

Salt and pepper tops of scallops. Bake at 400 degrees for 20 minutes. Serve at table in baking dish.

SIMPLY BAKED SCALLOPS

Wash scallops, wipe dry and place in a shallow baking dish. Salt and pepper scallops. Pour milk into pan to the depth of about ½-inch. Bake at 400 degrees for 20 minutes. Serve with baked potatoes, scalloped tomatoes, celery for an easy supper or dinner.

★This tartar sauce is good to serve with the baked scallops or any fish where it is needed.

TARTAR SAUCE

1 cup mayonnaise
½ teaspoon minced onion
½ teaspoon minced parsley
¼ cup finely chopped dill pickles
2 tablespoons chopped stuffed olives
1 teaspoon vinegar
Dash of black pepper

Combine, refrigerate in covered jar. Serve on piece of lettuce leaf.

SCALLOP SAUTE MONTAUK

Coat 1 pound scallops with:
¼ cup flour
½ teaspoon salt
Bit of black pepper

Cook in ¼ cup melted fat in frypan over low heat until lightly browned and tender.

Heat and Pour Over:

2 tablespoons melted butter
2 tablespoons lemon juice
1 teaspoon grated lemon rind
1 tablespoon chopped parsley

Serves 4.

SCALLOP CASSEROLE

½ pound scallops
½ pound haddock
1 can frozen shrimp soup
Buttered crumbs

Cut scallops in half. Cook halved scallops and haddock for 5 minutes, in salted boiling water.

Place scallops and haddock (which you will separate into bite-size pieces) in a buttered casserole. Pour unfrozen shrimp soup over the fish. Top with buttered coarse crumbs. Bake 30 minutes at 350 degrees.

DOWNEAST SCALLOPS

1 pint scallops
1 tablespoon butter or margarine
1 tablespoon flour
1 teaspoon dry mustard
1 tablespoon diced onion
1 tablespoon diced green pepper
1½ cups milk
1 cup grated American cheese
1/3 can tomato soup
1 small bottle stuffed olives

Cut scallops into quarters. Put scallops into saucepan, cover with cold water. Add salt. Bring to boiling point over a high heat and cook slowly for 5 minutes.

Melt 1 tablespoon butter or margarine in saucepan. Add chopped green pepper and diced onion. Cook slowly, until soft. Add flour and dry mustard. Add milk slowly. Cook over a low heat until thickened. Add 1 cup grated American cheese and the tomato soup. Add chopped, stuffed olives and cooked scallops. Pour into casserole, top with buttered crumbs.

Bake 30 minutes at 350 degrees. Make this ahead of time, it is better if it has had a chance to ripen. Just be sure it is at room temperature before putting it into oven, then it is cooked enough at the end of 30 minutes. Serves 4.

SAVORY SCALLOPS SERVED ON TOAST

1¼ pounds scallops
1 teaspoon vinegar
2 tablespoons butter
2 tablespoons flour
1/3 cup mayonnaise
½ teaspoon thyme
Salt to taste
Buttered toast

Parboil scallops in water that does not come quite up over them. Add vinegar. Keep water just under boiling, cook scallops just until they turn white. They cook quickly and overcooking toughens them. Drain and reserve the liquor.

Cut scallops into quarters. To scallop liquor add enough water to make 1 and 1/3 cups liquid in all.

Melt butter in separate saucepan, add flour, stir and blend. Add scallop liquor gradually, continuing to stir and cook over low heat. Add mayonnaise slowly, as soon as sauce thickness. Add cut-up scallops, thyme and salt. Heat through but do not boil. After combining all ingredients it will be best to keep this in top of double boiler over water kept just under boiling point. Serve on toast or in toast cups. This recipe serves 4 or 5. You might increase the amount of liquid to 2 cups, increase flour and butter to 4 tablespoons, use ½ cup mayonnaise, use same amount of scallops, and serve 6.

SHRIMP

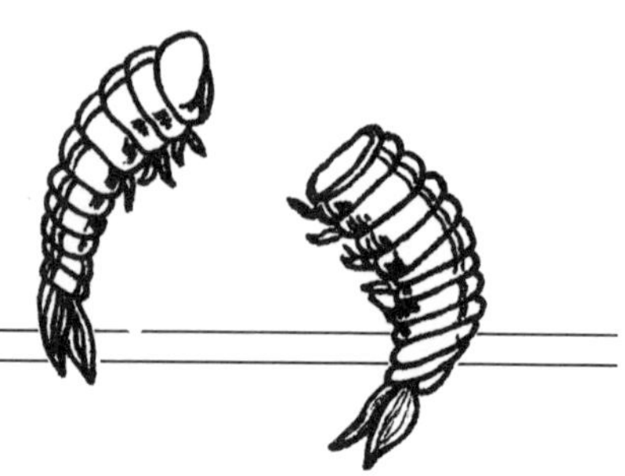

★ Signs of the times! Up to now, most books featuring Maine recipes have not included Maine shrimp but the Maine seafood industry now is harvesting millions of pounds of shrimp from the Gulf of Maine.

You will find Maine shrimp in three forms, canned, fresh, and frozen. If you are cooking Maine shrimp it helps to know you will end up with about half of what you start with. If a recipe calls for two cups of cooked shrimp, which is about one pound, then you will start with two pounds of raw shrimp in the shells.

The secret of the delicate flavor and texture of Northern shrimp is in its preparation. If you cook Maine shrimp, the rule is the same as for fish—Cook It Short. Maine shrimp are very accommodating, they do not need to be deveined.

HOW MUCH MAINE SHRIMP TO BUY

If you buy shrimp in the shell, you will get about half of what you start with. Two pounds of shrimp in the shell will give you one pound of the shrimp.

A one-pound package of frozen shrimp will yield 2 cups of shrimp, either fresh or frozen.

TO COOK MAINE SHRIMP IN SHELL

Wash shrimp. Break off heads using your fingers. Use a covered kettle and about 1 inch boiling, salted water. Place shrimp in kettle. Cover, bring back to a boil. Cook not more than 2 minutes after boiling point is reached. Drain, cool, remove shrimp meat by peeling off shells.

TO COOK SHRIMP MEAT

Place shelled out shrimps in about ½ cup boiling water, to which has been added salt and a small amount of lemon juice or vinegar. Cover, bring back to steaming point. It takes not more than one minute of cooking for peeled, raw shrimp. If you would protect its delicate flavor, do not overcook.

FREEZING MAINE SHRIMP

The heads are snipped off, using your fingers. Wash shrimp in salted water, place shrimp in plastic container, cover tightly and into the freezer they go. That's it, nothing else. You freeze them in the shell, which acts as a protection and keeps them from drying out.

No brine, nothing else. A container of quart size will hold about 60 Maine shrimp. No need to thaw shrimp before cooking. Just drop the frozen shrimp into inch of boiling water, return to boil and cook three minutes.

MAINE SHRIMP CASSEROLE

8 slices bread, buttered and cubed
½ pound sharp cheese, cut up fine
2 cups cooked Maine shrimp
3 eggs, well beaten
2½ cups milk (1 can cream of celery soup may be substituted for 1 cup milk)
½ teaspoon salt

Alternate layers of bread cubes, cheese and shrimp (starting with bread cubes) in a buttered casserole. Beat eggs thoroughly, add milk and salt, pepper too if you wish. Mix well and turn over the contents of casserole. Bake 1 hour at 325 degrees. Serves 4 generously.

★ Out-of-state jumbo shrimp are perfect for "baked stuffed". I think our friend from Pittston who shared her "company" recipe with us was more than generous, for everyone says it is the "best ever" method.

BAKED STUFFED SHRIMP

Buy frozen jumbo shrimp. (Allow 4 to a serving.)
Thaw them. Drain them.
Flatten shrimp in a buttered shallow baking pan.
Top with following dressing:
1 cup rolled cracker crumbs
1 cup finely crushed potato chips
1 stick butter or margarine melted
1 pint scallops, put through food grinder, raw.
Season with garlic salt. onion salt just a dash celery salt
Enough milk to make light and fluffy dressing.

Put generous amount of dressing on each flattened - out shrimp. This is enough for 16 to 20 jumbo shrimp. Sprinkle generously with grated Parmesan cheese.

Bake at 350 degrees about 20 minutes or until shrimp meat has turned white.

SEAFOOD NEWBURG

½ pound scallops
1 pound frozen Maine shrimp
¾ pound haddock
½ cup butter
4 tablespoons flour
2 cups milk
3 egg yolks
1 teaspoon salt
A shake or two of paprika
1 tablespoon lemon juice
6 tablespoons sherry

Cook the scallops, frozen Maine shrimp and haddock, taking care not to overcook. Drain. Prepare sauce as follows: melt butter in saucepan, add flour, mix well; add milk slowly, continuing to stir and cook over low heat until sauce thickens. This will take about 5 minutes.

Beat egg yolks. Add small amount thickened sauce to egg yolks. Blend, then slowly add egg yolk mixture to remaining sauce. Still using low heat, cook until sauce thickens. Add seasonings, add lemon juice and wine. Carefully fold in cooked fish. Turn mixture into a buttered 2-quart casserole. Top with buttered crumbs. Bake at 350 degreees about 20 minutes or until bubbly. Serves 6.

CANNED SEAFOOD CASSEROLE

One 6½ ounce can crabmeat
One 6½ ounce can lobster
One 5 ounce can medium shrimp
3 cups cooked rice
½ teaspoon pepper
1 can cream of celery soup
1 cup milk
2 tablespoons minced parsley
½ cup shredded cheddar cheese
½ cup buttered crumbs

Pick over crabmeat and lobster meat, if you can find the canned lobster meat. It is still being canned in Maine but is hard to find. You may just substitute another can of shrimp. Leave shrimp whole, devein if necessary. Mix cooked rice, soup mixed with milk, parsley and pepper, then combine gently with the fish. Turn into 2-quart casserole. Top with shredded cheese mixed with buttered crumbs. Bake at 350 degrees for 30 minutes or until bubbly hot. Serves 6.

★In spite of popularity of fresh crabmeat salad rolls or, for that matter, of fresh crabmeat salad, probably there is no more popular use of fresh Maine crabmeat than the crab cake recipe that was chosen to appear in that first "State of Maine Best Seafood Recipes". These crabmeat cakes could hardly miss, especially when served with lobster sauce.

BOOTHBAY HARBOR CRAB CAKES

1½ cups crabmeat
3 eggs, separated
1 cup cracker crumbs or soft bread crumbs
½ teaspoon salt
Dash of pepper
¼ cup melted butter
2 teaspoons lemon juice
1 teaspoon minced green pepper
1 teaspoon minced celery

Mix crabmeat, beaten egg yolks, crumbs, melted fat and all seasonings. Blend thoroughly. Fold in stiffly beaten egg whites. Turn mixture into 4 well-greased custard cups. Set them in a pan of hot water and bake at 375 degrees for 25 minutes. Unmold and serve with this lobster sauce.

LOBSTER SAUCE

To 1 cup hot medium white sauce add ½ cup finely cut cooked lobster. Heat well and pour over hot crab cakes.

ESCALLOPED CRABMEAT AND OYSTERS

1 2/3 cups crabmeat, or 1 can crabmeat
1 pint oysters
2/3 cup butter or margarine
1/3 cup flour
1 pint rich milk
1 1/3 cups fine bread crumbs
Salt and pepper

Make a white sauce of 1/3 cup margarine, 1/3 cup flour, salt, pepper and pint rich milk.

Clean oysters. Pick over crabmeat, removing all thin, flat bones. Either fresh or canned crabmeat is delicious.

Cook crumbs in remaining 1/3 cup of margarine, until crumbs are brown.

Grease casserole and arrange layers of white sauce, flaked crabmeat, oysters and crumbs. Top with crumbs. Bake at 350 degrees for 30 minutes. Serves 6.

CRAB SOUFFLE

1 can or ½ pound fresh crabmeat
4 slices bread, diced
½ cup finely diced celery
½ small onion, minced
1 tablespoon diced pimiento
¼ cup mayonnaise
1½ cups milk
2 eggs, beaten
½ cup cream of mushroom soup
Freshly grated cheese

Dice bread, place half in buttered 1½ quart casserole. Spread crabmeat over this. Mix mayonnaise, celery, onion and pimiento; turn over crabmeat. Mix milk, beaten eggs

★The Maine cook who gave me this recipe operated a restaurant in Gardiner. The good food served by this cook and her husband will long be remembered. Another of her recipes appears in my first cookbook. It wouldn't seem right not to share her Seafood Rarebit with you in this book. At the time she gave me this recipe, she said, "I have used this recipe for years. It is especially good to make ahead for a late supper. It is good warmed up."

SEAFOOD RAREBIT

In top of double boiler:
Melt 2 tablespoons butter or margarine
Add 2 tablespoons flour
½ teaspoon dry mustard
Salt and pepper to taste

Stir in:
1 cup finely cut sharp cheese
½ cup finely chopped green pepper
1 egg, beaten
¾ cup light cream or milk

Stir and cook until smooth and thick, over boiling water.

In a separate saucepan heat 1 can undiluted tomato soup with a pinch of soda until soup gets bubbly. Add to mixture in top of double boiler, continuing to stir. Then add:

1 can shrimp or 1 cup fresh shrimp
Or, 1 can crabmeat or 1 cup fresh crabmeat
Or 1 can lobster meat or 1 cup fresh lobster
Or one 8-ounce can tuna
Or 1 cup any cooked fish

Isn't this an easy recipe to concoct? So many choices, too. You may serve this rarebit on crackers, rusk, toast points, rice, or in your favorite manner.

This is spelled rarebit, not to be confused with a Welsh Rabbit, which of course is something else.

MAINE LOBSTER

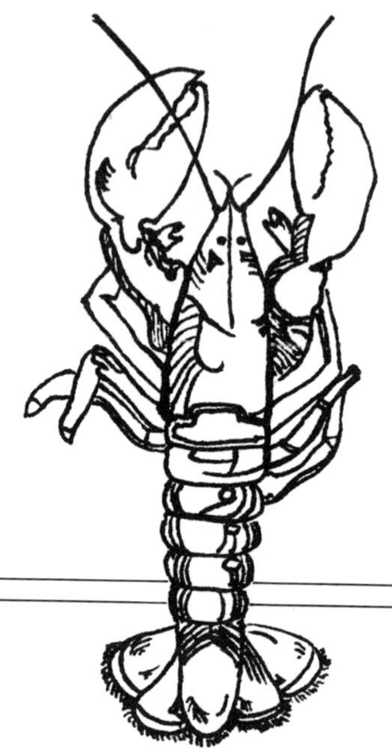

★Growing up on New Meadows River taught a lot of things about the cooking of fish and seafood.

My uncle who lived with us down on the farm often did masonry work for the late Robert P. Tristram Coffin. He would bring my uncle home in the late afternoon and I have seen them sit out in the yard for a couple of hours just talking.

Do you suppose that is where we got the idea of using such a small amount of water in boiling Maine lobsters? In his book, "Mainstays of Maine," Mr. Coffin says lobsters should always be steamed and that one-half cup boiling water will do for a whole kettle of lobsters. I don't go quite that far, but I will suggest 2 inches of boiling water. As a Bailey Island fisherman observed, "you only want to cook 'em not drown 'em".

STATE OF MAINE BOILED LOBSTER

Have 2 inches boiling water in a large kettle. Add 1 to 2 tablespoons salt, depending upon number of lobsters and size of kettle. Plunge live and kicking lobsters in, head downward. Cover kettle, bring quickly back to steaming point. Time 16 to 18 minutes for 1-pound size and 18 to 20 minutes for 1¼ to 1½ pound lobsters.

Remove from water and place each lobster on its back to drain. Serve hot with melted butter. If you serve them cold, use mayonnaise in place of melted butter.

HOW TO EAT LOBSTER

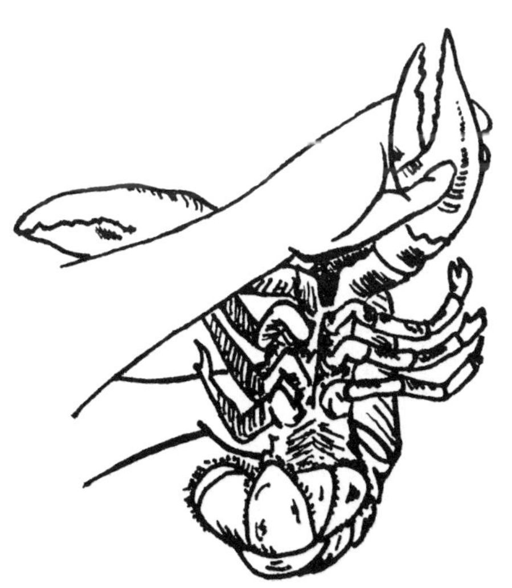

1. Twist off the claws.

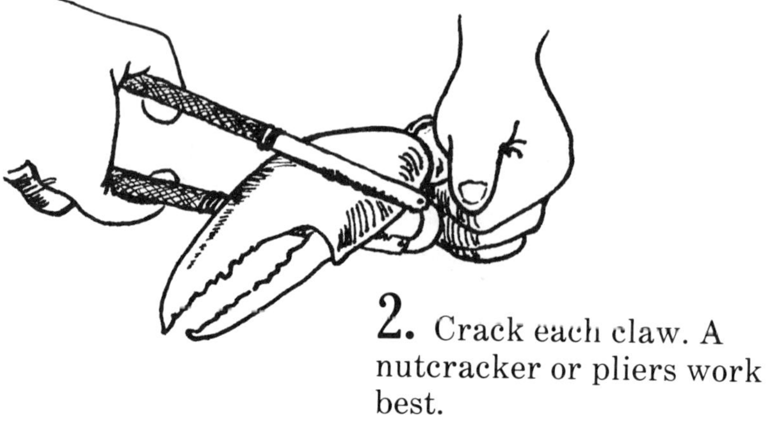

2. Crack each claw. A nutcracker or pliers work best.

3. Separate the tail piece from the body by arching the back until it cracks.

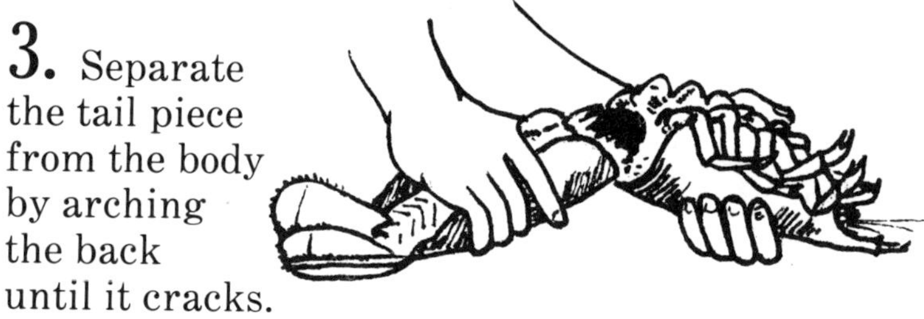

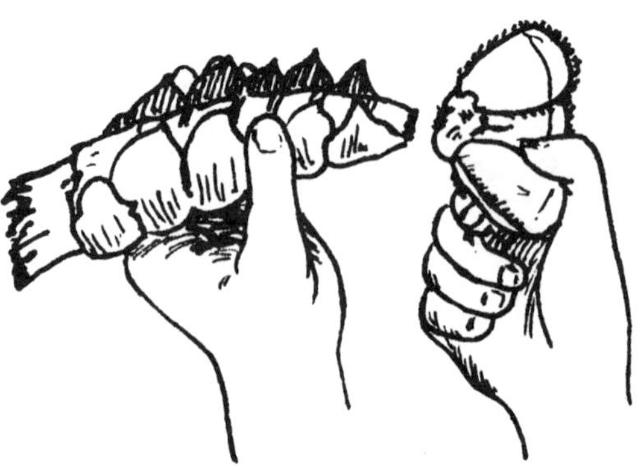

4. Break off the flippers by bending them back.

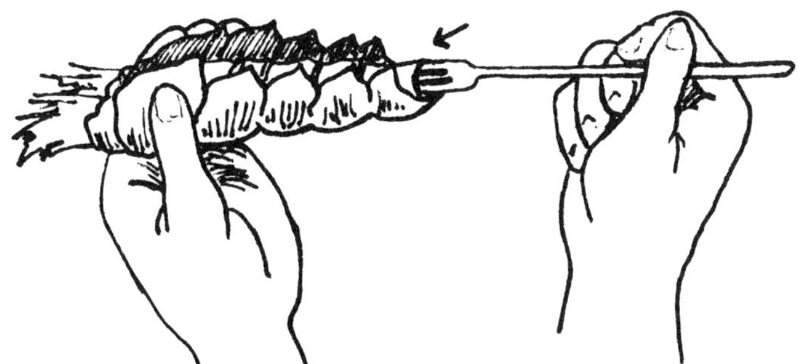

5. Insert a fork where flippers broke off and push tail meat

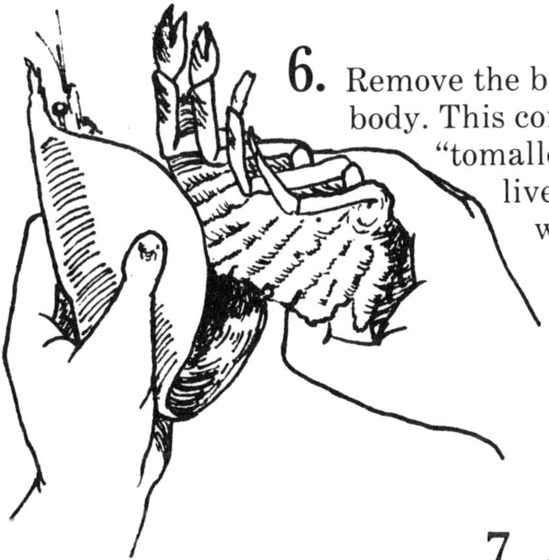

6. Remove the back from the body. This contains the "tomalley" or the lobster's liver. It turns green when it's cooked and is considered by many to be the best eating of all.

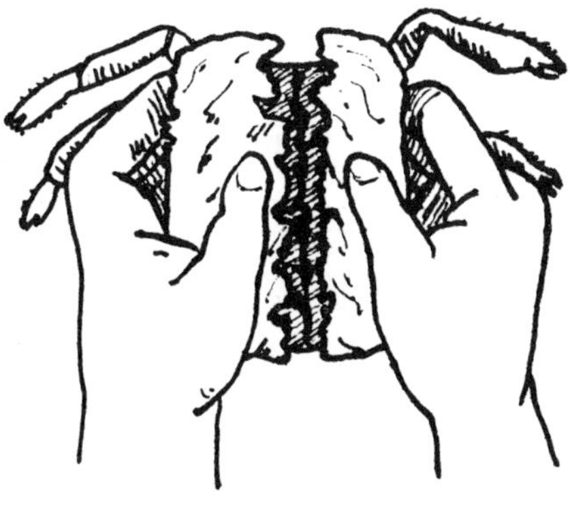

7. Open the remaining part of the body by cracking apart sideways. The small claws are excellent too. The meat is sucked out, much like a straw.

BAKED STUFFED LOBSTER

★Did you ever split a **live** lobster? Probably you have not intended to, but if it is carefully explained, perhaps you will be encouraged to fix baked stuffed lobster. Most cookbooks say, "Split a lobster". Just about then you probably decide you will have yours boiled. So, step by step, let's learn how to split, clean, stuff and bake a live Maine lobster.

TO SPLIT A LIVE LOBSTER

Place the lobster on its back. Cross the large claws over its head and hold firmly with your left hand. This is it! Make a deep, quick incision with a sharp pointed knife and draw the knife quickly down the entire length of the body and tail.

TO CLEAN LOBSTER

Spread the lobster flat. Using a teaspoon, remove the tomalley. This will go into the stuffing. So will the coral or roe, if it happens to be a female lobster. The next step is to break the intestinal vein where it is attached to the end of the tail. Use the handle of the spoon to do this. Before you remove this vein there is another step. Use your fingers to remove the sac or stomach (a lobster's stomach is under its head). Using two fingers, remove this sac in one fell swoop. As you do this it will break the other end of the intestinal tract. Now, use the teaspoon handle again and complete the removal of this tract.

Make sure the cavity is cleaned out, you may do this by holding under running cold water. Turn lobster over and allow to drain. It is now ready for stuffing.

STUFFING FOR LOBSTER

For 8 lobsters use following amount:

½ pound butter, melted
2 cups dried bread crumbs, ground fine (make this a generous amount)
2 teaspoons Worcestershire sauce
A little salt
Tomalley and coral, too

Mix all together. Fill cavity of lobster with the stuffing, using a spoon for this. Divide the amount of stuffing among the number of lobsters you are baking, using amounts above as a guide. With this amount of butter in stuffing, no need to "dot" any on top. For a drier stuffing, use more bread crumbs.

Place stuffed lobsters in foil-lined pan. Alternate heads and tails so they will fit better in pan. Bring edge of foil up over end of tail of each lobster. Press foil, so it secures end of tail firmly to edge of pan. If you do not do this, tails are apt to curl up as they bake. Remove plugs from claws if you wish.

Bake at 325 degrees for 50 minutes, depending upon size of lobsters.

★ Watching the popularity of a recipe grow is interesting pastime. I remember when my Farmington roommate used this recipe for Maine lobster casserole for the very first time. She served it to the directors of the Central Maine Power Company for a luncheon at the annual meeting a long, long time ago. Since then the popularity of the casserole has grown and grown. After all, when you have a group of men telling about the goodness of a casserole, you can be certain it is.

LOBSTER CASSEROLE

3 tablespoons butter
1 pound cooked lobster meat
3 tablespoons flour
¾ teaspoon dry mustard
3 slices white bread, crusts removed
2 cups rich milk, part cream
Salt and pepper to taste

Cut lobster in bite size pieces and cook slowly in butter to start pink color. Do not cook too long or too fast or it will toughen. Remove lobster meat. Add flour mixed with seasonings to fat in pan. Add rich milk slowly. Cook, stirring constantly until thickened. Add lobster and bread torn into small pieces. Turn into buttered casserole. Top with a few buttered crumbs and bake at 350 degrees for about 30 minutes or until bubbly and delicately browned. If desired, a tablespoon or two of sherry may be added to the mixture. Serves 4.

★ Without question, I have more requests for lobster Newburg than any other lobster recipe. A tablespoon of lemon juice in the following recipe does not mask the flavor of the lobster and is a variation from the usual sherry in a Newburg. You might prefer using a tall can of evaporated milk in place of the light cream, it will avoid the worry of curdling.

LOBSTER NEWBURG

2 cups lobster meat cut in medium-sized pieces
4 tablespoons butter
1 tablespoon flour
1 cup light cream
2 egg yolks, beaten
1 tablespoon lemon juice
¼ teaspoon salt
Paprika

Melt 3 tablespoons butter, add lobster meat and cook slowly to start the pink color, use a low heat for doing this. In another saucepan, melt the remaining tablespoon butter, add flour, salt, a dash of paprika. Add cream or evaporated milk, stirring constantly, cook over low heat until thickened. Remove from heat, turn into beaten egg yolks. Turn back into pan, return to heat, stir again until thickened. Add the heated lobster and lemon juice, serve at once on toast points. Serves 4.

AN AMAZING LOBSTER NEWBURG

¾ pound lobster meat
½ cup sherry
2 tablespoons butter
2 tablespoons flour
2 hard-cooked egg yolks
1½ cups cream, plus
¼ cup milk
Pinch of nutmeg
Pinch of cayenne pepper
Salt to taste

Soak cooked lobster meat cut in bite-size pieces in sherry for 2 to 3 hours in refrigerator. Make a paste of softened butter, flour and the hard-cooked egg yolks that have been rubbed through a sieve. Use a heavy iron skillet, combine this paste with cream, milk, nutmeg and cayenne pepper. Add salt later.

Use a low heat, stir sauce until quite thick. Drain sherry from lobster meat, add to sauce, continue stirring and cooking until it is thick. Add lobster meat. Stir until hot.

Amazingly, this is better made the day before serving and stored in the refrigerator. Heat and serve on toast points.

TO MAKE TOAST CUPS

Use fresh bread. Cut off crusts. Use muffiin tins. Press each slice into tins so that 4 points stand up. No need to brush with butter. Bake at 400 degrees for 15 minutes or until brown. If you need several, allow to cool in pan, remove to cookie sheet. Continue to do this until you have number needed. The toast cups will hold their shape. Slide cookie sheet into oven for reheating.

FISH

COD

★Ever wonder what Maine mothers and grandmothers served with baked beans on Saturday night before the days of the hot dog? Many of course, felt baked beans, brown bread, pickles with cake for dessert was ample. Yet if men worked hard all day on Saturday as they did not too many years ago, most housewives felt baked beans needed an additional dish to make Saturday night supper more hearty. Codfish cakes filled this need.

If there were any fish cakes left over, then they were sure to appear at Sunday morning breakfast with warmed-up baked beans.

I remember fish cakes best when my mother had prepared them and placed them on a platter ready to be fried to a golden brown. They looked all "whiskery".

FISH CAKES

1 box or 1 pound salt codfish
4 or 5 medium size potatoes
¼ teaspoon pepper
1 egg

Soak salt codfish overnight in water to cover. In morning, drain fish, add peeled potatoes, sliced about ½ inch thick.

Add about 1 cup cold water, bring to a boil together and cook until potatoes are done. About 15 minutes.

Drain in a colander and return to saucepan. Mash fish and potatoes together, add whole egg, pepper and beat with a silver fork. With a tablespoon, scoop up the mixture and shape with the silver fork so that the cakes are "whiskery". Slide onto a platter. Place in a cool spot until ready to fry.

To fry, have 1/4 inch hot melted shortening in skillet. Fry crusty gold on each side, turning once.

★ Probably no old-style Maine dinner brings more favorable comments than a salt codfish dinner. The salt codfish placed on a platter with pork scraps, surrounded with boiled potatoes of uniform size and small buttered or sliced beets, the fish topped with a plain or egg sauce, not only looks good, it is good.

SALT COD DINNER

1 pound salt cod
6 medium-sized Maine potatoes
6 medium-sized beets
4 tablespoons all-purpose flour
1/4 pound salt pork
2 cups milk
1/4 teaspoon pepper

Soak salt codfish overnight to freshen it. If time is a factor, then place dried salt fish in a kettle, add about 1 quart cold water. Heat this to just about the boiling point, but do not boil. Pour off this water and do it all over again. You probably will want to do this a third time, too. Taste fish to be certain it is not too salty.

After freshening fish by either method, simmer it just below the boiling point, until fish is tender. This will take only a few minutes. Remember, this fish should never be boiled, it makes it tough. The fish is done if it will flake when broken.

Boil the potatoes. Boil and dice or slice the beets or use canned beets.

Wash the ¼ pound salt pork, then dice. Cook salt pork very slowly in a frying pan over low heat. Drain the pork and return about 4 tablespoons of the fat to frying pan.

Add 4 tablespoons flour to the fat and stir. Add pepper. Add milk slowly, stirring constantly so that the gravy will be smooth. Add a little salt if necessary. Keep this gravy hot. At this point, the cooked salt cod may be added to this gravy or served in the following manner:

TO SERVE SALT COD

Place freshened, cooked fish on a hot platter. Place the crispy bits of fried salt pork on top of the fish. Make a red border of the diced or sliced beets around the fish. Serve the gravy and the cooked potatoes separately. If you prefer, the gravy may be poured over the fish, then the crispy salt pork sprinkled on top of this.

Better serve johnnycake with this, hadn't you? Serves 6, by the way.

FISH ROE

If you get a hankering for a dinner of fish roe it is a sure sign spring is on its way.

Roe, with the exception of shad roe or any other small roe should be parboiled. The roe is then fried or broiled, as desired. Bacon is good served with roe.

To cook roe, wash it, drop it into boiling, salted water. Use a teaspoon of salt. Add 1 tablespoon vinegar or lemon juice. Simmer covered 5 minutes for a medium sized roe or 10 minutes for a large roe.

Drain, cover with cold water, drain again. Carefully remove fine membrane covering the roe. Roe may be mashed and fried or broiled in a large cake or made into smaller cakes.

My best success comes from frying it in bacon fat, loose, then as it cooks make it into a cake. Fry until lightly browned.

★ In case you wondered where the name finnan haddie originated, it gets its title from the reputation of haddock cured around Findon, Scotland. For a long time I used to think of it as strictly a New England kind of fish. Today, it isn't even haddock that is used for smoked fillets — the high price makes this prohibitive. Usually cod or hake is used and it is called smoked fillets. Several processing plants along the Maine coast smoke fillets. They are delicious and naturally are used like finnan haddie. Occasionally you will find finnan haddie in our markets. Sometimes the fillets have not been smoked but have been dipped in a colored, smoky liquid to give the same flavor. These are lighter in color and the color will come off in milk or water.

SMOKED FILLET CASSEROLE

1 to 1½ pounds smoked fillets
Water or skim milk to cover fish
2 tablespoons margarine or butter
½ cup diced green pepper
1 small onion, diced
4 tablespoons flour
¼ teaspoon salt
2½ cups milk

Cut fish in three or four pieces, place in large saucepan, cover with water or skim milk. Place over a low heat, let stand until fish is ready to flake. Drain. This could have been leftover cooked fillets, in which case you would eliminate this part of directions. While fish cooks, melt margarine or butter in saucepan, add green pepper and onion and cook over low heat until soft. Add flour, stir until smooth. Add salt and the milk, using a low heat; stir constantly until thickened.

Place the flaked fish in a buttered 2-quart casserole. Make certain any bones are removed. Turn the thickened sauce over the fish. Top with buttered crumbs. Bake at 350 degrees for about 25 minutes. Serves 6.

★Smoked fillets appeal to many, if they just happen to appeal to you, then this finnan haddie casserole will be a favorite.

FINNAN HADDIE CASSEROLE

3 pounds finnan haddie (smoked fillets) soaked in cold milk to cover
3 cups cooked rice
2 cans Welsh rarebit or 2 cans cheese soup or 2 packages frozen Welsh rarebit
2 cups milk (to mix with rarebit)
Grated cheese
Buttered crumbs

This recipe will serve 8, generously. Place smoked fillets in a large saucepan. Cover with cold milk and soak for 1 hour. Place pan on heat and simmer until fish flakes. Spoon milk over fish occasionally as it heats. Discard this milk as it's too salty to use.

Cook enough dry rice so that you will have 3 cups of cooked rice. Mix the 2 cups of milk with Welsh rarebit and combine with 3 cups cooked rice.

Use a large casserole, buttered. With a slotted spoon lift the smoked fish keeping it in as large flakes as possible and place in buttered casserole. Lightly mix with the cooked rice and cheese mixture. Grate American cheese over top. Top with buttered crumbs. Bake at 350 degrees for 30 minutes. I think of this recipe as being adult fare.

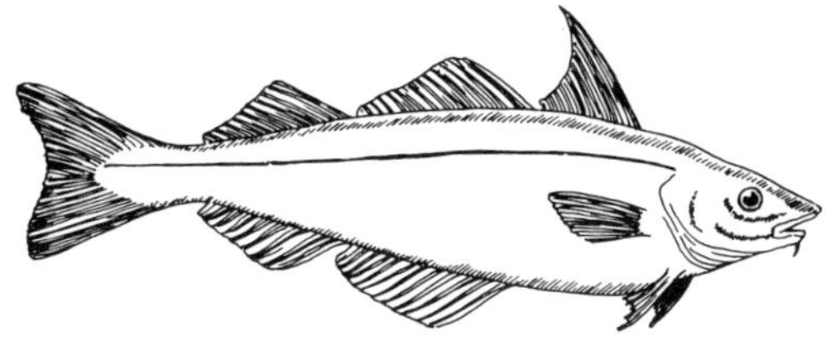

HADDOCK

BROILED HADDOCK

Wipe the number of pieces of haddock you need, then prepare by dipping each serving piece in a dish containing some commercially prepared Italian dressing. Then, roll each piece in cornflake crumbs and lay on broiler pan. After each piece has been prepared in this manner dot each piece with margarine.

Place under broiler and broil 10 minutes on a side. Season after broiling.

★ Basically, Maine fish recipes are very simple. This is because freshly caught fish needs little to enhance its flavor. Salt and pepper, maybe a little onion, parsley or lemon juice. There is one important rule in cooking any fish and that is—Cook It Short. Keep in mind to cook fish only until it is tender, but no longer. This preserves its delicate flavor and texture.

ROLLED HADDOCK FILLETS

6 haddock fillets
Butter or margarine
1½ cups soft bread crumbs
2 tablespoons minced onion
2 tablespoons minced parsley
Salt and pepper
Hot water to moisten dressing

Salt haddock fillets, spread with dressing; roll up and secure with toothpicks. Bake at 450 degrees for 30 minutes. Serve with egg sauce.

BAKED HADDOCK

2 pounds fish fillets
½ teaspoon salt
¼ teaspoon paprika
Black pepper
Lemon juice

SAUCE
2 tablespoons butter
2 tablespoons flour
Salt and pepper
1 tablespoon dry mustard
1 cup milk

TOPPING
½ cup buttered crumbs
1 tablespoon parsley

Lay fish fillets in a shallow pan. Season with the salt, pepper, paprika and lemon juice. Make sauce of butter, salt and pepper, flour, dry mustard and milk, cooking in a saucepan over a low heat, stirring constantly until thickened. Pour this sauce over seasoned fish. Top with buttered crumbs. Bake at 350 degrees for 35 minutes. This recipe serves 6.

★Haddock Smother is not a chowder but I suggest you serve it in soup plates. It is as old-fashioned as any recipe in this cookbook. If haddock is not available, substitute cod or hake. You will not notice much difference, anyway. You will like this on a chilly summer's day as well as the coldest day in winter.

DOWN EAST HADDOCK SMOTHER

Buy amount of fish necessary for your size family. Wipe with paper toweling and salt lightly. Cook in as little water as possible in a shallow, broad-bottomed saucepan. Use cold water, bring to a gentle boil and cook until just done. "Cook it short," as we say when cooking fish. Add enough milk to just cover fish; add salt and pepper.

Cover top of fish with crackers. Originally, we used Kennedy's Commons, no longer available. You may be able to find common crackers; if not, use whole unsalted crackers, thicker than saltines. These crackers should be soaked lightly in cold water before being placed on top of the cooked fish. Do not use milk for soaking the crackers. It would toughen them. Use a slotted spoon to lift them from the water and place them on the fish.

Push the crackers down into the milk. Dot tops with butter; allow to simmer a few minutes, using a low heat. Serve in soup plates, topped with a dash of paprika.

A tossed salad will be the right accompaniment for this.

★This recipe has deep meaning for men of the Woodfords Club in Portland. Russ Foster, the steward there, finds the popularity of this delicious fish very gratifying. After all, it is his own recipe. He shared it with us in my Cooking Down East column and now everyone in Maine can know about Famous Baked Haddock.

RUSS FOSTER'S FAMOUS BAKED HADDOCK

You can adapt this recipe according to the number of people you will be serving. For four people, use a 7 x 11-inch casserole. Rinse and wipe 1½ to 2 pounds fresh haddock fillets. Place a layer of haddock in bottom of buttered casserole. Add a second layer of fillets, making certain you place them on the bottom layer so a thick end comes on top of a thin end of the fillet beneath. You will serve the cooked fish in squares, so you see what you need to achieve. There should be an even thickness of fish all over the casserole. Squeeze fresh lemon juice all over the fish. Do this between each layer, too. Add salt and pepper. Cover top with buttered crumbs. Try using half cracker crumbs and half packaged seasoned crumbs. Bake at 350 degrees for ½ to three-quarters of an hour. Serve in squares.

For two people, use 1 pound fillets and a loaf pan for baking to get desired thickness. Three pounds of fillets will serve 8 people generously. This is good company fare. May be prepared ahead, then brought from refrigerator an hour ahead of baking time.

CRISP OVEN FRIED FISH

1½ pounds fish (cusk, hake or haddock)
3 cups cereal flakes
1 tablespoon salt
1 cup milk
2 tablespoons melted butter

Cut fish into serving pieces, allowing about ¼ pound fish per person. Roll cereal flakes into fine crumbs. Add salt to milk. Dip fish in milk, then in crumbs, arrange on well-buttered baking sheet. Dribble melted butter over top of fish. Bake at 500 degrees (this is correct) for 15 to 20 minutes.

BAKED FISH STICKS

2 pounds fish sticks
Salt and pepper
½ stick margarine, melted
6 tablespoons flour
Milk

Cut fish sticks into 6 servings. Salt and pepper each piece. Place in buttered shallow 7 x 11-inch pan. Mix flour with melted margarine so it is a paste. Add bit more flour if needed. Spread paste on top of each serving of fish. Pour milk in pan so it comes up around fish. Bake at 350 degrees about 45 to 50 minutes or until the fish flakes when tested with a fork.

FISH IN CHEESE SAUCE

3 tablespoons margarine
3 tablespoons flour
½ teaspoon salt
¼ teaspoon pepper
½ teaspoon dry mustard
1½ cups milk
One 8-ounce package sharp cheddar cheese
2 pounds haddock, cooked
Buttered crumbs

Melt margarine in saucepan. Add flour, salt, pepper and dry mustard. Blend together, then add milk slowly. Cook over low heat, stirring constantly until thickened. Cut up cheese, add to sauce, stir until melted. Fold in cooked fish. Cook fish gently in salted water, using a low heat until it flakes. Separate into bite-size pieces before adding to sauce.

Turn into 2-quart casserole, top with buttered crumbs. Bake at 325 degrees about 25 minutes. If you prefer, this may be cooked in top of double boiler, kept hot over simmering water, served in toast cups. Serves 6.

FISH SPENCER

6 fish sticks (choose nice fat ones)
1 egg
2 tablespoons milk
Salt and pepper
Butter or margarine
Cornflakes, rolled

Wipe fish sticks, season, dip in egg which has been slightly beaten and combined with milk; roll in cornflakes. Place in well-buttered baking dish, dot generously with butter or margarine. Bake about 30 minutes at 450 degrees.

★ A long time ago, a summertime friend at South Harpswell gave us this recipe for a fish loaf. "Guaranteed to make anyone a fish eater," she stated. She is absolutely right, too. Served with a butter sauce or a frozen shrimp soup sauce, it makes a very special dinner.

SHANTY FISH LOAF

2 cups flaked cooked fish (preferably haddock)
1½ cups soft bread crumbs
½ teaspoon baking powder
2/3 cup finely chopped celery
1/3 cup finely minced onion
1 tablespoon lemon juice
1 cup milk
1 tablespoon minced pimento
1 tablespoon finely chopped green pepper
Salt and pepper

Mix all ingredients lightly. Turn into buttered bread tin. Bake at 350 degrees for 1 hour.

Serve with desired sauce, such as a butter sauce with capers added. Frozen shrimp soup, heated undiluted makes an excellent sauce, or your own favorite cream sauce for a fish loaf. Serves 6.

★This casserole recipe includes scallops as well as fish, also frozen cream of shrimp soup. This is another do ahead recipe which is well liked by all cooks.

LUNCHEON SEAFOOD CASSEROLE

1 stick margarine, melted
1 cup cracker crumbs
1 cup scallops, cut small and parboiled 5 minutes
1 pound haddock or other fish, cooked gently and flaked. Save 2/3 cup of the liquor from haddock
1 can undrained minced clams
1 can frozen shrimp soup, thawed
Small onion, finely minced
Salt and pepper

Mix margarine and crumbs. Set aside. Combine cooked scallops, haddock, clams and onion. Using one-half of the crumb mixture, combine with fish. Season lightly.

Combine thawed soup and haddock juice, mix with fish, taste again for seasoning. Turn into 2-quart casserole. Refrigerate if you wish. Before baking, cover top with remaining buttered crumbs. Bake at 350 degrees for 40 minutes. Serves 8.

HALIBUT

BAKED HALIBUT

1½ pounds halibut
¾ teaspoon salt
Dash of pepper
1 tablespoon butter
1 tablespoon flour
1 cup boiling water
2 teaspoons lemon juice
1 tablespoon prepared mustard
½ cup dried bread crumbs
1 tablespoon butter

Place halibut steak in a shallow baking pan. Sprinkle fish with salt and pepper. Cover with sauce, made as follows: melt butter, add flour, prepared mustard, lemon juice and boiling water, cook over low heat stirring constantly until thickened.

Melt remaining tablespoon butter and mix with bread crumbs, cover fish evenly. Bake at 350 degrees about 40 minutes.

★It was the longest time ago that I used this excellent method for cooking halibut in my column, "Cooking Down East." The recipe came from the Maine Department of Sea and Shore Fisheries.

HALIBUT BAKED IN A COVERED DISH

2 pounds halibut, preferably in one chunky piece
2 tablespoons soft butter or margarine
¼ teaspoon pepper
¼ teaspoon paprika
Dash of salt
Fresh grating of nutmeg

Have fish at room temperature. Combine butter, pepper, salt, paprika and nutmeg. Rub both sides of fish with it. Place fish in an ovenproof dish, cover with foil. Bake at 325 degrees until fish flakes; time depends upon shape. The general rule is 20 minutes for 1-inch thick fish, 30 minutes for 2-inch thick and 35 minutes for 3-inch thickness. 2 tablespoons water may be added while cooking. Place fish on a hot platter.

For a tasty sauce melt 3 tablespoons butter or margarine, add 2 tablespoons chopped pickles, 1 teaspoon chopped parsley, 1 teaspoon chopped chives and ½ teaspoon salt. Pour over fish. Makes 4 to 6 servings.

★ Halibut loaf is a prize-winning recipe long used by Maine cooks. Another recipe you can use year around with perfect results each time. Well-liked by both men and women, it is just the sort of easy dinner for a special family occasion or for guests. Halibut loaf has a lot of satisfying goodness and delicate taste.

HALIBUT LOAF

1 pound boned, uncooked halibut, ground or chopped fine
1 pint bread crumbs (use soft centers of a white loaf)
1 cup cream
Mix bread crumbs with cream to make a smooth paste

To uncooked, finely ground fish, add:
1 teaspoon salt
½ teaspoon celery salt
Combine seasoned fish and bread and cream mixture
Beat whites of 4 eggs and fold into fish mixture

Line a 9- by 5-inch loaf pan with waxed paper and grease paper well. Pour mixture into loaf pan. Pour some water into a more shallow pan. Place pan of fish mixture into this and bake at 350 degrees for 45 minutes. When loaf is baked, turn onto a platter and remove waxed paper. Serves eight.

Now comes the special part about this loaf, the type of sauce you serve on it. Tomato sauce is delicious, but so is almond sauce or lobster sauce. Here are recipes for all three.

TOMATO SAUCE

One No. 2 can tomatoes
Add:
1 slice onion
1 teaspoon salt
½ teaspoon sugar
¼ teaspoon pepper

Cook for 15 minutes, using a low heat. Strain. Melt 4 tablespoons butter or margarine, add 2 tablespoons flour.

Add the strained tomato, slowly. Cook over a low heat until thickened, stirring constantly. Serve hot.

ALMOND SAUCE

Brown ¼ pound chopped or slivered almonds in 2 tablespoons butter. Add 2 tablespoons flour and blend. Add ½ teaspoon salt and ¼ teaspoon pepper. Add 1 pint thin cream slowly, stirring constantly, cook until thickened. Serve hot.

LOBSTER SAUCE

3 tablespoons butter or margarine
3 tablespoons flour
1 teaspoon salt
¼ teaspoon pepper
1 cup milk
½ cup cream
1 to 1½ cups cooked lobster meat

Melt the butter or margarine, add flour and seasonings, stir until blended. Add milk and cream slowly, cook over a low heat, stirring constantly until thickened. Add chunks of lobster meat. Heat carefully, making sure the sauce does not boil.

HAKE

★ Corned hake is an old Maine dish. It is remembered by many and it is amazing how Maine families cling to serving this old-fashioned dinner. It is delicious and you will like serving it to your own family. Corned hake, boiled potatoes, butter gravy or, if you prefer, salt pork gravy is good any time of year. Use buttered beets for a vegetable. Just maybe you will want to chop some raw onions, place in a bowl, sprinkle a bit of sugar on top, pour vinegar over them, allow to set. Come dinnertime, pass the bowl, and sprinkle a few onions on top of the hake.

Always popular, hake is growing in popularity in Maine. It is a less expensive fish, delicious used in a chowder. In fact, you would use it as you do any fish. Try dipping hake fillets in beaten egg, then crumbs, as this holds the fish together for pan frying. You may buy fillets or round hake, meaning it is whole. Corned hake is usually available in your fish market, but you are going to feel very old-fashioned if you corn your own.

DIRECTIONS FOR CORNING HAKE

Two and one-half to three pounds of hake will serve four people amply and should leave enough fish to make hash or fishcakes. Buy either fillets or a piece of round hake. Wipe fish, place in dish, sprinkle with salt on both sides, cover, place in refrigerator eight hours or overnight. Before using, drain fish but do not wash.

CORNED HAKE AND BOILED POTATOES

Pare potatoes, place in large saucepan with small amount of water. Do not salt. Cover pan and boil potatoes until nearly done; place drained hake fillets on top of potatoes, add dash of pepper if you wish. Cover, bring back to steaming point; lower heat, allow to simmer 10 to 15 minutes longer. If it is chunk of corned hake, allow about 20 minutes, test for doneness, taking care to cook only until it "flakes."

Try out (fry) salt pork scraps if you like, using fat to make salt pork gravy. The crispy pork scraps can be sprinkled on top of fish when served. If you prefer a butter gravy, why not make it as our Gardiner neighbor used to do it. These directions came from her.

BUTTER GRAVY

Scald one pint of milk in top double boiler placed over boiling water. Add ½ teaspoon salt to milk. Mix 2 tablespoons flour with cold water so mixture is thin, add to scalded milk, stirring constantly until thickened. Add piece butter or margarine, pepper to taste, and one cut-up, hard-cooked egg. Many oldtime cooks used to simply beat up the raw egg in a cup, add it to the thickened gravy, stir until well blended. Then, tiny pieces of the cooked egg were all through the gravy. Leftover gravy may be added to fish hash or fish cakes.

★ Rarely will you find a recipe for fish hash in any of today's cookbooks. Probably you do not need a recipe. Maybe you would rather make fish cakes. But if you happen to have leftover fish and potatoes, either boiled or mashed, why not get out your heavy frypan and make hash. My mother was a great hand to make fish hash, probably because we ate a lot of fish. I'm sure she did not have a recipe.

FISH HASH

1½ cups cooked fish
2 cups mashed or boiled potatoes
¼ teaspoon pepper
Salt to taste
1 egg, beaten
2 tablespoons margarine

Combine leftover fish and mashed potato, or if it's leftover boiled potato, then chop fine with fish. Add pepper and salt, mix with beaten egg. Add some dry mustard if you wish. Melt 2 tablespoons margarine in heavy frypan, add hash, cover pan. Use foil if your pan has no cover. Fry, using a medium heat until browned on the bottom. Fold over and serve very hot. Serves 4. Corn meal muffins, sliced carrots and a tossed salad are good with fish hash.

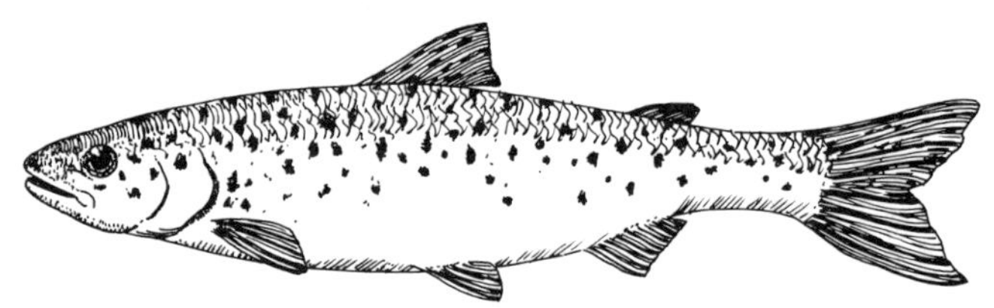

SALMON

★ It is a Maine tradition on the Fourth of July to serve fresh salmon, fresh green peas and new potatoes for your family dinner. The custom persists and I have questions like, "My mother cooked her piece of fresh salmon in cheesecloth and it was steamed. How do I do this, so I may carry on the tradition in my own family?" Of course you want to do this. Chances are there was a vegetable garden in your own back yard, where your father took great pride in raising "peas for the Fourth." Mine did. Green peas are still ready for the Fourth in Maine.

It means planting them by Patriot's Day — April 19th. It is a kind of silent contest in Maine among gardeners. Any man is happy to announce, "We're having peas from our garden for the Fourth!" They will not be new Maine potatoes at this time of year but you will probably serve boiled potatoes. They will be new and they will have come from out-of-state.

FRESH SALMON FOR THE FOURTH

THE AMOUNT TO BUY

When buying fresh salmon allow one-half to three-quarters of a pound per person. To refrigerate, remove the fish from the wrappings, place on a plate or platter with a piece of wax paper over it. This allows for circulation of air. If storing cooked fish in your refrigerator, it should be completely covered.

TO PREPARE FOR COOKING

As with all fish, fresh salmon neeeds little seasoning. The flavor of fish is so delicate that seasonings and sauces tend to take away from it.

Keep in mind that lemon juice and fish are old time partners. If no fresh lemon juice is available, then add vinegar to the water in which fish is cooked. This makes the salmon more firm and helps to preserve the color, too. Salt is the only other seasoning needed.

TO STEAM FRESH SALMON

In a covered pan, put enough hot water to come up fairly well around the fish. Add one-half teaspoon salt and one tablespoon fresh lemon juice (or vinegar) to each quart water used. Wrap salmon in cheesecloth and lower into the water. Cover pan, bring to steaming point. Reduce heat and allow to simmer 8 to 10 minutes per pound.

If fish is cooked too rapidly, it loses both flavor and food value. So remember to cook just under the boiling point. When tested with fork and salmon is flaky, drain, carefully remove the cheesecloth and arrange the salmon on a heated platter. Serve immediately with boiled new potatoes, fresh peas and a bowl of creamy egg gravy.

EGG GRAVY

4 tablespoons margarine
4 tablespoons flour
½ teaspoon pepper
½ teaspoon salt
2 cups milk
3 hard-cooked eggs

Melt margarine in saucepan using a low heat. Stir in flour, salt and pepper. Add milk gradually while continuing to stir; cook over a low heat until thickened and smooth. Add shelled hard-cooked eggs that have been cut up or chopped. The gravy may be further enhanced by adding a bit of minced fresh parsley and a bit of fresh lemon juice.

You may prefer fresh salmon baked in milk. Salt the fish, place in shallow pan, add about ½ inch milk. Bake at 375 degrees, allowing 12 minutes to the pound or until fish "flakes" when tested with a fork. Use uncovered pan for this.

★ It might be a can of salmon kept in the refrigerator that will solve your summertime dinner problem. A one-pound can of salmon will serve 4. Salmon colored pink, medium-red or red all has the same food value but if you decide to do this with a can of salmon, then red has the greatest eye appeal. Turn contents of can into a bowl, remove skin and bones, separate the salmon into big chunks, arrange on lettuce on a platter with wedges of lemon and dollops of mayonnaise. No muss, no fuss. The chilled salmon served with potato salad and frozen peas cooked by the following method is a simple dinner to prepare.

TO COOK FROZEN PEAS

Use pan with tight fitting cover and only enough cold water to cover bottom of pan. Turn frozen peas into pan, add salt, cover pan. Bring to steaming point, making certain it is a forceful steam; lower heat and cook 10 minutes. Drain most of water from peas, draining it all, if you wish. Add piece of butter or margarine, salt and pepper to taste and a pinch of sugar. Reheat, serve very hot. This is not according to most package directions. Many cooks like to add cream to the peas after they have been seasoned.

BROILED SALMON STEAKS

4 to 6 salmon steaks
Salt
Pepper
Butter
Parsley

Wipe fish with a damp cloth; sprinkle with salt and pepper.

Place fish on greased broiler rack about 4 inches from heat; broil until fish is delicately browned. Turn carefully and broil on other side until fish flakes easily when tested with a fork. Serve fish hot with parsley butter sauce.

PARSLEY BUTTER SAUCE

1 tablespoon butter
1 tablespoon minced parsley
Few grains pepper
1 teaspoon lemon juice
¼ teaspoon salt

Cream butter with parsley, salt, pepper, and lemon juice. Spread the sauce over the cooked fish.

★Back when I was doing cooking schools this was one of my favorite recipes. Or you could make a salmon wiggle.

SALMON LOAF

1 large can red salmon
½ teaspoon salt
¼ teaspoon paprika
¼ teaspoon pepper
3 tablespoons lemon juice
3 egg whites
¼ cup melted butter or margarine
3 egg yolks
1½ cups firmly packed soft bread crumbs
1½ cups scalded milk

Remove skin and bones from salmon and mash very fine. Mix salmon, paprika, pepper, salt and lemon juice, melted butter, beaten egg yolks and bread crumbs. Add hot milk, fold in stiffly beaten egg whites. Pour into greased loaf pan. Bake at 375 degrees for 1 hour. Serve with egg sauce. Serves 8.

EGG SAUCE

4 tablespoons butter
4 tablespoons flour
½ teaspoon salt
Dash of pepper
2 cups milk
2 hard-cooked eggs

Melt butter, add flour, seasonings and blend well. Add milk slowly, stirring constantly. Cook over low heat until thickened. Cut hard-cooked eggs in small pieces and add.

SALMON WIGGLE

4 tablespoons margarine or butter
4 tablespoons flour
¼ teaspoon pepper
½ teaspoon salt
2 cups milk
1 can red salmon
1 can peas, drained, or 1 package frozen peas, cooked

Prepare cream sauce by melting margarine, adding flour, salt and pepper. Stir until smooth. Add 2 cups milk, gradually. Cook over low heat, stirring constantly, until smooth and thickened. Add drained peas. Add salmon that has been picked over, bones and skin removed. Keep salmon in fairly large pieces. Serve on buttered toast, toast cups, patty shells, on crackers or baked potatoes. Serves 4 to 6.

★ As soon as it was learned I had another cookbook underway the questions started. The one asked most often was, "Will you have lots of casserole recipes?" Of that you may be certain. Like this recipe using a can of salmon.

SALMON SURPRISE

1 tall can red salmon (A 1-pound can)
1 can cream of mushroom soup
Same amount milk measured in soup can
One 4-ounce package potato chips
3 slices onion, minced fine
½ cup sliced ripe olives

Prepare salmon by removing skin, bones and breaking into large pieces. Place half this salmon in buttered 7 x 11-inch casserole. Sprinkle a bit of onion over this, half of the ripe olives, half of the potato chips that have been crumbled. Mix soup and milk and turn half of this over potato chips. Repeat but save other half potato chips for topping of casserole. Bake at 350 degrees for 45 minutes. Serves 4.

SARDINES

★ Maine sardines — the little fish with the big flavor. Tins of sardine are what you take along on a trip — in your survival box. No family should ever go away from home for a few days and not include a small carton of foods for any emergency. Tins of Maine sardines take up so little room and they pack so much needed food value. Don't forget the box of salted crackers.

The many ways to use sardines are unlimited. They combine well with cheese, lemon juice, onions, tomatoes, bread, milk, potatoes. So there is no limit to what you may achieve if you have tins of Maine sardines stored in your cupboard.

DELUXE MAINE SARDINE SANDWICH

3 cans (4 oz.) Maine sardines
6 frankfurter rolls
Barbecue sauce or cocktail sauce
3 tablespoons butter or margarine
6 slices Swiss cheese
6 onion slices, if you wish

Cut rolls almost in half, lengthwise. Place opened rolls on a cookie sheet, spread with melted butter, place under broiler. Toast, spread other side with butter, toast, also. Lay 3 sardines on each sandwich half, spoon barbecue sauce over sardines. Add onion slices if you wish, lay slice Swiss cheese on top. Place under broiler until cheese melts. Serves 6. These are served hot and you will find this one of the most delicious sandwiches you will ever eat. If you do not have a broiler, toast the rolls, assemble sandwich, then bake at 425 degrees for 12 to 15 minutes.

★ If Maine sardines right out of the can suit you best, then you are not interested in doing much else to them. A "squirt" of lemon juice, salt and pepper or a dash of Tabasco is what people like best. A tin of Maine sardines is a good traveling companion and they are good for you.

Just in case you want to do something else with Maine sardines, then these two recipes that have been popular will please you, too.

TOSSED SARDINE SALAD

2 cans Maine Sardines
½ cup salad oil
¼ cup lemon juice
1 tablespoon sugar
1 teaspoon salt
1 teaspoon paprika
1 teaspoon dry mustard
¼ teaspoon dry pepper
½ teaspoon Worcestershire sauce
1 large head lettuce
½ cup sliced green pepper
1 cup sliced celery
1/3 cup sliced stuffed olives

Drain sardines. Add this oil to other oil. Place oil in tightly covered jar along with lemon juice, sugar, salt, paprika, dry mustard, black pepper, Worcestershire sauce. Set aside while preparing salad ingredients. Save out five sardines for garnish. Break remaining sardines into quarters and toss together with lettuce, green pepper, celery and sliced stuffed olives in salad bowl. Toss salad with dressing and garnish with whole sardines.

SARDINE STUFFED TOMATO CUPS

2 tins, Maine sardines
1/3 cup diced celery
1 tablespoon diced onion
2 tablespoons salad dressing
4 drops Tabasco sauce
½ teaspoon Accent
4 small tomatoes

Open the tins of Maine sardines, reserve 4 whole sardines. Drain. Add celery, onions, salad dressing, Tabasco sauce and Accent. Mix well. Peel tomatoes and scoop out small section, fill cavity with sardine mixture. Top with whole sardine.

MAINE SARDINE DIP

One 4-ounce can Maine sardines
One 8-ounce package cream cheese
1 tablespoon milk
2 teaspoons grated onion
1 tablespoon Worcestershire sauce
1½ tablespoons lemon juice
Salt and pepper to taste
2 tablespoons chopped parsley

Drain sardines, break into small pieces. Soften cream cheese, mix with milk. Combine all ingredients except parsley. Mix thoroughly. Chill. Sprinkle with parsley. Serve with chips, crackers or crispy raw vegetables.

SMELTS

It is hard to realize that a born and bred State-of-Mainer could forget such an important part of wintertime eating in our state. After all, you only need to take a ride on a winter's day and see the smelt shacks that dot the frozen rivers in many parts of Maine. If men, and women too, arrive at work on winter mornings looking a little bleary-eyed, it is almost certain they spent many hours in a smelt shack fishing for the next night's supper. If you catch your own, they are that much sweeter.

TO PREPARE AND COOK SMELTS

Place a piece of wax paper on a cutting board, place smelt on it, cut off head with a sharp knife. Cut along abdomen, using kitchen shears, remove entrails. Using your thumb, completely clean the smelt. Leave tail on, but use shears to cut off fins. Rinse fish thoroughly, wipe dry.

This is where Maine cooks differ in the way they cook

smelts. You may fry them, broil them or bake them. You may roll them in a mixture of seasoned cornmeal. You may combine flour with cornmeal and season it. You may use a commercial preparation for dredging the fish. Or you may leave them plain.

You may fry them in salt pork fat, in melted margarine or butter or in oil. If you fry them, do it gently on one side until done, then turn and complete the other side. If you decide to bake them, use a shallow, buttered pan, in a hot oven of 450 degrees, 5 minutes on a side. If you prefer, you may broil them.

Isn't it nice to have a choice? No matter how you cook them, they are delicious and very much a part of the wintertime scene in Maine.

SOLE

BROILED FILLET OF SOLE

Wipe fillets. Lay fish flat on aluminum foil in a broiler pan or shallow baking pan. Dot lightly with butter, season with salt and pepper. Place under broiler. Leave oven door ajar and broil about 6 or 7 minutes. Sole is thin and usually does not need to be turned during the broiling. Serve hot with wedges of lemon. If you do not have a broiler, then follow same procedure and bake at 400 degrees for 20 minutes.

★ This has to be one of my favorite ways of cooking fish—fillet of sole with oysters. It is expensive and takes a while to prepare but if you are looking for exactly the right recipe for guests, this has to be it. The Maine cook who gave it to me was chairman of the Maine Women's Golf

Association that year. She liked it, for it could be prepared ahead. We all like this, especially when guests are invited.

FILLET OF SOLE WITH OYSTERS

2 pounds fillet of sole
1 cup chicken broth
3 tablespoons butter
2 tablespoons lemon juice
1 quart fresh mushrooms, sliced
2 dozen oysters, plus liquor, or use Maine shrimp

Heat broth, butter and lemon juice, using a large skillet. When butter is melted add fillet of sole. Lay sole in broth, simmer just until tender, about 3 minutes. If pan does not hold all of sole, do separately, so you do not crowd it. Butter a 13 x 11-inch pan. Lay cooked fish in pan. Add sliced fresh mushrooms to broth, cover, cook about 5 minutes; remember mushrooms take very little cooking. Use canned, sliced mushrooms if fresh are not available.

Drain mushrooms, save broth. Arrange mushrooms on top of fish. Add 2 dozen oysters and liquor to broth and simmer long enough for edges of oysters to curl. If you use Maine shrimp, then simmer only until shrimp curl. Remove from broth, arrange on top of mushrooms. Measure broth. You should have 1 and ¾ cups; if not, reduce amount by simmering. You will make a sauce with this broth.

TO MAKE SAUCE

5 tablespoons butter
½ cup flour
1 and ¾ cups fish broth
1 cup light cream or evaporated milk
Salt and pepper to taste
6 tablespoons grated parmesan cheese
3 tablespoons minced parsley
1 tablespoon grated onion
1 cup buttered soft bread crumbs

Melt butter, add flour, blend together; add fish broth and light cream slowly, stirring constantly. Cook over low heat until thickened. Add cheese, parsley, onion, salt and pepper to taste. Pour over contents in casserole. Top with buttered soft bread crumbs. Bake at 350 degrees for 30 minutes or until bubbly. Serves 8.

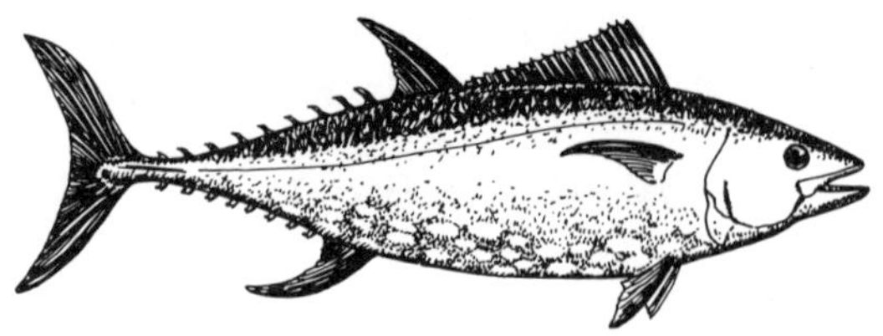

TUNA

★ The Bailey Island Tuna Tournament makes Maine tuna country. At Bailey Island during the summer months, it is not uncommon to have one or more tuna fish on the wharf daily being weighed and prepared for market. The appearance of fresh Maine tuna in our fish markets is a welcome sight. Usually low in price and considered a great treat, fresh tuna is served by Maine cooks as long as it is available.

TO COOK FRESH TUNA

Fresh tuna steaks are red and look exactly like beef steak. Again, "cooking it short" applies. Usually, Maine cooks fry fresh tuna or it is broiled. Remember, only until it changes color is enough. Because it is oily, many cooks parboil it first. You may prefer broiling it, under these circumstances, brushing it with melted butter or margarine and using fresh lemon juice for tartness and good flavor.

★Do you ever watch the way canned tuna disappears from the grocer's shelves? It makes you aware that it is a necessary part of meal planning, both from the economy standpoint and from its many uses; all easy ones, too. Tuna Divan does not sound State-of-Maine-ish but we like everything about it.

TUNA DIVAN

One 10-ounce package frozen broccoli stalks, cooked and drained
Two 6½-ounce cans white meat tuna, water-packed, drained, separated into large chunks
Fresh lemon juice
1 can cheddar cheese soup
Buttered crumbs or buttered croutons

Use a buttered 7 x 11-inch casserole. Place drained, cooked broccoli stalks in casserole. In a separate bowl, mix drained tuna, about 1 tablespoon lemon juice and the soup. Spoon this mixture over the broccoli. Top with buttered crumbs or buttered croutons. Bake at 350 degrees about 25 minutes or until bubbly. Serves 6.

TUNA-NOODLE BAKE

One 8-ounce package wide noodles, cooked and drained
One 6½-ounce can tuna, of your choice, drained
¾ cup milk
1/3 cup pimientos, diced
1 can cream of mushroom soup
For topping:
Crumbled potato chips

Have you learned about cooking macaroni products the easy way? For this amount of noodles, boil 1 quart water in covered saucepan. Add salt. Add noodles, stirring constantly; bring to a boil, continue stirring for 2 minutes. Cover pan. Remove from heat. Let stand 10 minutes. Stir, then drain. Easy? Never boils over, either.

Combine cooked noodles, tuna that has been cut-up, milk and soup that have been mixed together, diced pimiento, and add some pepper if you wish. No salt needed. Turn into buttered 1½ quart casserole. Top with crumbled potato chips. Bake at 350 degrees about 35 minutes. Serves 4.

Do you have a problem keeping pimiento once it has been opened? Simply turn some vinegar on top of it in jar, cover, place in refrigerator. It keeps for weeks.

★ A can of tuna in the cupboard is great insurance for all sorts of cooking emergencies. One of the first cooking schools I ever conducted was in the town of Limerick. During that series of three schools, this way of preparing tuna was used in an oven meal. It is a recipe that may be used just as given, yet if you do not have time to make the cheese swirls for the top, then serve the tuna mixture in toast cups, on crackers or as a shortcake using cornbread.

TUNA WITH CHEESE SWIRLS

3 tablespoons chopped onion
1/3 cup chopped green pepper
4 tablespoons margarine
1 teaspoon salt
A little black pepper
6 tablespoons flour
1 can chicken soup with rice
1½ cups milk
One 7-ounce can white meat tuna
1 tablespoon lemon juice

Melt margarine in pan. Add chopped green pepper and onion. Cook slowly until tender. Add salt, pepper and flour. Add chicken soup gradually, stirring constantly. Add milk and stir until thick and smooth. Add tuna and lemon juice. I usually add some chopped pimiento. Pour into a good-sized casserole. Cover with cheese rollups. Bake at 425 degrees for 25 minutes.

If you have prepared the creamed tuna ahead and it is stored in refrigerator, be sure it is warmed before putting cheese swirls on top. Otherwise the bottoms of biscuits will be under done.

CHEESE SWIRLS

2 cups flour
4 teaspoons baking powder
½ teaspoon salt
4 teaspoons shortening
2/3 cup milk
¾ cup grated American cheese
2 tablespoons chopped pimiento
Dash cayenne

Sift flour. Measure. Sift together into bowl with baking powder and salt. Cut in shortening. Add milk and mix lightly with fork. Roll into rectangular shape. Sprinkle with grated cheese and chopped pimiento and a dash of cayenne. Roll like jelly roll. Cut in slices and place over creamed tuna.

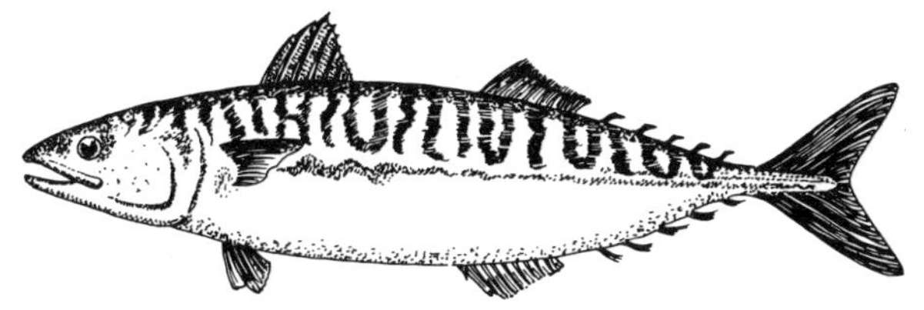

MACKEREL

★ Tuna is horse mackerel and this all leads up to one of Maine's most popular fish — mackerel. Best of all is tinker mackerel. If you have ever fished for mackerel, found your boat in a "school," only had to drop your line with a jig hook over the side of the boat, hauling them in so fast you stood ankle-deep because the half-barrel was overflowing, then the joy of sharing and eating them is very great.

You can buy them in your markets, from someone who might call at your door, or maybe the fishman still calls in your town. If a friend calls with an offer of mackerel he has caught, then be sure to accept them, for his joy is sharing them.

If you have never eaten tinker mackerel, I'm sorry. Tinkers are the babies, weighing not over a pound. There isn't another fish like it. They are simple to cook. Just allow enough per person.

TO COOK TINKER MACKEREL

They may be fried or broiled and they may be baked in milk the way people like to cook larger mackerel. Cook them as simply as possible. No sauce of any kind, for they are too delicious as they come out of the frypan or from the broiler.

Use salt pork fat or butter or margarine. Cook them just as they are or roll them in flour or a combination of flour and cornmeal. Cooks like the commercial preparations too, for dredging fish for frying. Season with salt and pepper.

Once the tinker mackerel have been cleaned, you may decide to cook them whole, because of their size. Yet, many people like to split them. No matter what you do, keep the cooking simple.

★Baking mackerel in milk is the Maine way of cooking this popular fish. Again, no other seasoning except salt and pepper and the moistness of milk; oh well, a few dots of butter.

MACKEREL BAKED IN MILK

Once the mackerel has been split and cleaned, arrange in a glass baking dish. Season with salt and pepper, dot with butter, pour milk in pan so it comes up to depth of fish but not over it. Bake at 350 degrees for 40 minutes.